BANT Methodology: The Secret Formula for Qualifying Leads and Exploding Sales

Copyright © 2024 Reginaldo Osnildo
All rights reserved.

PRESENTATION

INTRODUCTION TO BANT: THE FOUNDATION OF LEAD QUALIFICATION

BUDGET : ASSESSING FINANCIAL CAPACITY

AUTHORITY: IDENTIFYING DECISION MAKERS

NEED: UNDERSTANDING CUSTOMER REQUIREMENTS

TIMELINE (DEADLINE): UNDERSTANDING THE CUSTOMER'S URGENCY

APPLYING BANT IN DIFFERENT SALES SCENARIO

EFFECTIVE COMMUNICATION USING BANT

OVERCOMING OBJECTIONS WITH THE HELP OF BANT

INTEGRATING BANT WITH OTHER SALES STRATEGIES

TOOLS AND TECHNOLOGIES TO SUPPORT BANT

TRAINING AND SKILLS DEVELOPMENT IN BANT

30-DAY ACTION PLAN TO IMPLEMENT BANT

REGINALDO OSNILDO

PRESENTATION

Welcome to the beginning of a transformative journey in the world of sales! If you are a sales professional or part of a team dedicated to this competitive and dynamic universe, you know that success does not come by chance. It is necessary to constantly improve your techniques, strategies and, above all, the way you qualify your leads. This is where our book, **"BANT Methodology: The Secret Formula for Qualifying Leads and Exploding Sales** ", comes into play to be your ally in this process.

This is not just another book about sales. Here, you will find a refined synthesis of traditional knowledge combined with an updated perspective on the BANT method (Budget, Authority , Need , Timeline), a classic and extremely effective tool for qualifying leads. But we go further: we decode and adapt this method so that it fits perfectly with the demands and challenges of the current market.

Throughout this book, you will be guided by chapters that complement each other and unfold in a fluid and logical way, always with the aim of making your reading not only informative, but also inspiring and practical. From the introduction to the BANT framework, through the detailed analysis of each of its components (Budget, Authority , Need , Timeline), to the application of these concepts in different sales scenarios, effective communication, overcoming objections, integration with other sales strategies sales, and much more.

Each chapter has been carefully crafted with you in mind: we want you to feel invited to explore the entire book, progressively deepening your understanding and skills. Furthermore, we recognize the importance of technology and digital tools in supporting the sales process, which is why we have dedicated a special space to discuss how you can make the most of them.

This book is the result of in-depth research and my experience in the field of sales, with the purpose of bringing you valuable content that synthesizes cutting-edge knowledge and contributes significantly to your professional growth. Here, you will find not just theory, but a series of practical tips and a concrete action plan for the next 30 days, designed to help you implement the BANT method into your sales routines, elevating your lead qualification skills to a new level.

I invite you to embark on this journey of discovery and improvement. Get ready to dive into the BANT universe, where the objective is clear: maximize your results in sales qualification, allowing you and your team to not only reach, but exceed your goals.

Let this book be your guide to sales success. Let's start?

In the next chapter, " **INTRODUCTION TO BANT: THE FOUNDATION OF LEAD QUALIFICATION** ", you will take the first step toward understanding the foundation on which we will build all of our work. Are you ready to transform the way you qualify your leads and maximize your sales efficiency? So, turn the page and let's go on this journey together!

Yours sincerely

Reginaldo Osnildo

INTRODUCTION TO BANT: THE FOUNDATION OF LEAD QUALIFICATION

As we delve into the essence of this book, it is essential to start with the foundation that supports the entire sales lead qualification structure: the BANT method. Originating from a concept developed by IBM in decades past, BANT has become a timeless tool for sales professionals around the world. But what exactly is BANT and why does it remain so relevant in today's digital age?

BANT is an acronym for **Budget , Authority , Need and Timeline** . Each letter represents an essential criterion for determining the viability and potential for converting a lead into a customer. Let's explore each of them:

- **Budget:** Refers to the lead's financial capacity to purchase your product or service. Understanding your lead's budget is crucial to adapting your value proposition according to financial limitations or opportunities.

- **Authority :** Identifies who has the decision-making power over the purchase. In many organizations, especially in B2B sales, the purchasing decision is a complex process involving multiple people or departments. Knowing who you're talking to can save time and target your efforts more effectively.

- **Need :** Understanding your lead's specific needs is the heart of consultative selling. Without knowing in depth what your potential customer needs, it is impossible to offer a truly valuable solution that justifies the investment.

- **Timeline:** Time is a critical factor in sales. Knowing when the customer intends to make a purchase can help you adjust your approach, whether speeding up the sales process or nurturing the relationship with the lead until they are ready to buy.

WHY IS BANT SO EFFECTIVE?

The BANT method has stood the test of time for a simple reason:

it is practical. By qualifying leads based on these four criteria, you can focus your efforts on the most promising contacts, optimize your sales process and, consequently, improve your conversion rates. In a world where time is a valuable resource, knowing where to invest your energy can make the difference between a successful quarter and one of stagnation.

ADAPTING BANT TO THE CURRENT REALITY

Although BANT has its roots in a perhaps simpler sales context, its essence is perfectly applicable to the complexities of today's market. The difference is how we adapt and interpret each element of BANT to meet the expectations and behaviors of modern consumers. For example, decision-making authority may now be dispersed among multiple influencers within an organization, or even outside of it, on social media and online forums.

In this chapter, we explore the foundation on which we will build our understanding and application of BANT. In the following chapters, we will dive into each of the BANT components, detailing strategies and techniques for you to effectively apply in your sales interactions. You will discover not only how to adapt your approach to each criterion, but also how to use BANT flexibly and creatively, aligning it with the nuances of contemporary consumer behavior.

Now that you understand the fundamental structure of BANT and its relevance in the lead qualification process, you are ready to move forward and explore each aspect in detail. In the next chapter, " **BUDGET: ASSESSING FINANCIAL CAPACITY** ", we will discuss how to identify and address your lead's budget effectively, ensuring that your solutions align with their financial possibilities and needs.

Get ready to deepen your knowledge and skills, becoming a master in the art of qualifying leads. Let's go together on this journey to maximize your sales results, one step at a time. Turn the page, and let's continue exploring the universe of BANT Descomplicado.

BUDGET : ASSESSING FINANCIAL CAPACITY

Understanding a lead's budget is critical for any sales professional. This chapter is dedicated to uncovering how you can assess the financial capabilities of your prospects and, more importantly, how to adapt your sales approach to align with their financial capabilities. After all, knowing the available budget directly influences the way we present our solutions, helping to create proposals that not only meet customer needs, but also respect their financial limitations.

THE IMPORTANCE OF KNOWING THE LEAD'S BUDGET

Understanding your lead's budget allows you to adjust your value proposition to match the customer's expectations and financial capabilities. This not only means avoiding wasting time on negotiations that will never materialize, but also building a relationship of trust and transparency from the beginning. By demonstrating that you respect your lead's financial limitations and are willing to work within them, you establish a solid foundation for future interactions and negotiations.

HOW TO IDENTIFY THE LEAD BUDGET

- **Ask directly:** Although it may seem obvious, many professionals are hesitant to ask directly about the budget. However, approaching the matter openly and professionally can save both parties time and effort. Phrase your questions in a way that demonstrates your intention to understand the lead's needs and limitations to offer the most appropriate solutions.

- **Observe indirect signs:** The lead will not always be willing or able to provide clear information about their budget. In these cases, it is important to pay attention to indirect signals, such as comments about previous costs, past purchasing decisions or even the level of urgency demonstrated in relation to the solution sought.

- **Use CRM tools and market data:** Customer Relationship

Management (CRM) tools and market data analysis can offer valuable insights into a lead's budget potential, based on information such as company size, industry performance and even previous purchases.

ADAPTING YOUR SALES APPROACH TO THE LEAD'S BUDGET

Once you have a clear understanding of your lead's budget, the next step is to adapt your sales approach accordingly. This could mean:

- **Customize packages and offers:** Develop product or service package options that can be adjusted to suit different budget ranges. This not only increases your chances of closing a sale, but also demonstrates flexibility and understanding of the customer's needs.

- **Emphasize ROI (Return on Investment):** For leads with restricted budgets, it is crucial to highlight the value your solution offers in terms of return on investment. Focusing on how the product or service can save money in the long term, increase efficiency or boost revenue can help justify the cost against the available budget.

- **Negotiation of payment terms:** Be flexible on payment terms. Offering extended payment plans, discounts for cash payments or other special conditions can make the difference in closing a sale within the lead's budget.

With a clear understanding of your lead budget and strategies for adapting your value proposition, you are prepared to move forward in the lead qualification process. However, identifying the budget is only one part of the equation. The next step, and the topic of our next chapter, is to understand " **AUTHORITY: IDENTIFYING DECISION MAKERS**" within your lead's organization.

In this next chapter, we'll explore strategies to ensure you're talking to the right people capable of making or influencing the purchasing decision. After all, aligning your solution to the lead's budget is only effective if you're presenting it to those who actually have the power to say "yes."

Get ready to dive into the nuances of identifying and engaging decision makers. This knowledge not only speeds up the sales process, but also significantly increases your chances of success. Let's continue this journey together, turning every opportunity into a successful sale.

AUTHORITY: IDENTIFYING DECISION MAKERS

Advancing on our journey to master the BANT method, we come to a crucial aspect that can define the success or failure of a sale: identifying the decision makers. In this chapter, we'll explore effective strategies to ensure you're talking to the right person, the one who has the authority to make or influence the purchasing decision. Understanding who has the decision-making power is vital, because even with the right budget and a clear need, if your solution doesn't get into the hands of the right people, the chances of conversion can be significantly reduced.

THE IMPORTANCE OF IDENTIFYING DECISION MAKERS

In many organizations, the purchasing decision is not made by a single person, but is the result of a collaborative process that may involve multiple stakeholders, each with their own concerns and evaluation criteria. Identifying and involving decision makers early on is crucial to:

- **Speed up the sales process:** By avoiding wasting time with intermediaries who have no decision-making power, you can focus your efforts where they really matter.

- **Personalize your approach:** Understanding the specific motivations and responsibilities of decision makers allows you to tailor your communication to address their particular concerns.

- **Increase the probability of success:** When your solution is presented directly to those who can say "yes", the chances of closing a sale are significantly greater.

HOW TO IDENTIFY DECISION MAKERS

- **Preliminary research:** Use professional social networks such as LinkedIn, corporate websites and industry publications to identify who holds leadership and decision-making positions in areas relevant to your solution.

- **Strategic questions:** During your interactions with the lead, ask questions that can reveal the company's decision-making structure. For example, ask how previous similar decisions were made and who was involved in the process.

- **Observation and active listening:** In meetings and presentations, observe the dynamics between participants. Who asks the most questions? Who seems to have the final say? Active listening during these interactions can provide valuable clues.

- **Ask for recommendations:** In some cases, it may be helpful to ask your current contact directly to recommend the best person to discuss your proposal. This can be done in a respectful manner, emphasizing your desire to ensure information gets into the right hands.

ENGAGING DECISION MAKERS

Identifying decision makers is just the first step; effectively engaging them is the next challenge. Here are some tips:

- **Personalize your message:** Based on your research, tailor your message to resonate with the specific interests and needs of decision makers.

- **Demonstrate value:** Emphasize how your solution can solve specific problems, improve processes, or contribute to company goals in a measurable way.

- **Make the decision easier:** Provide success stories, testimonials and data that can help mitigate perceived risks and facilitate the decision-making process.

Now that you know how to identify and engage decision makers, it's time to deepen our understanding of your leads' needs. In the next chapter, " **NEED: UNDERSTANDING CUSTOMER REQUIREMENTS** ," we'll explore techniques for uncovering your customers' true needs, allowing you to customize your solutions even more effectively.

Deep understanding of customer needs is key to presenting your solution not just as an option, but as the obvious choice. Get ready to dive into strategies that will transform your sales approach, making it irresistibly aligned with your customers' wants and needs. Let's move forward, as each step takes us closer to maximizing our sales qualification results.

NEED: UNDERSTANDING CUSTOMER REQUIREMENTS

Delving even deeper into the BANT methodology, we arrive at an essential component that defines the effectiveness of our sales: Need. This chapter is dedicated to exploring how you can discover and understand your customers' true needs, a crucial step that allows you to customize your solutions in an effective and targeted way. Understanding what your customer really needs not only strengthens the value proposition of your product or service, but also establishes a deeper connection with the customer, demonstrating that you are genuinely interested in solving their problems and meeting their expectations.

THE IMPORTANCE OF UNDERSTANDING CUSTOMER NEEDS

Identifying customer needs goes far beyond listening to what they say they want. It involves careful analysis of the subtext, the circumstances, and even the unspoken problems that your solution can solve. This understanding allows:

- **Align your value proposition:** Make sure what you offer solves the customer's specific problems, increasing the relevance and impact of your solution.

- **Build lasting relationships:** By focusing on customer needs, you demonstrate empathy and commitment, key elements for building long-term trust and loyalty.

- **Differentiate yourself from the competition:** When you understand and meet customer needs more effectively than your competitors, you stand out in the market.

TECHNIQUES TO DISCOVER CUSTOMER NEEDS

- **Ask open-ended questions:** Start conversations that encourage the client to talk about their challenges, goals and concerns. Questions like "What do you think could be improved about your current process?" or "What are your main goals for this year?" can reveal deep needs.

- **Active listening:** Pay attention not just to what is said, but how it is said. Body language, tone of voice and what is not said can offer valuable clues about the customer's true needs.

- Analysis of previous cases: Examine previous situations with similar clients to identify patterns of needs that may apply to the current case.

- Utilize customer feedback: Comments and reviews from existing customers can provide insights into common needs that you can anticipate in future negotiations.

CUSTOMIZING NEED-BASED SOLUTIONS

With a clear understanding of customer needs, you can now customize your solutions so that they resonate directly with what matters most to the customer. This involves:

- Adaptation of features and benefits: Highlight the aspects of your product or service that directly align with identified needs.

- Creation of personalized proposals: Prepare proposals that reflect an understanding of the client's specific needs, demonstrating how your solution is the best option to meet them.

- Providing relevant examples: Use case studies or testimonials that show how you met similar needs for other customers, increasing credibility and confidence in your solution.

Understanding your customer's needs is only part of the equation in effectively qualifying leads. The next component, " **TIMELINE (DEADLINE): UNDERSTANDING THE CUSTOMER'S URGENCY**", will equip you with strategies to determine the ideal timeline for purchasing or implementing your solution. Knowing when the customer is planning to act is crucial to adjusting your sales strategy and pressing at the right time.

This knowledge not only helps you sync your actions with

the customer's purchasing cycle, but also allows you to offer valuable support and information at a time when it's needed most. Get ready to explore how understanding and influencing your customer timeline can accelerate your sales and improve the effectiveness of your lead qualification. Let's move on to the next chapter, where every moment is an opportunity to get even closer to closing the sale.

TIMELINE (DEADLINE): UNDERSTANDING THE CUSTOMER'S URGENCY

Advancing the lead qualification journey using the BANT method now leads us to explore the "Timeline" or Deadline, an essential component that determines the urgency and timing of the customer's purchasing decision. This chapter focuses on how you can determine and influence your customer's timeline for purchasing or implementing a solution by adjusting your sales strategy to align with those timelines. Understanding the customer's timeline is not just about knowing when to act, but also about how your solution can perfectly fit into the customer's planning and temporal needs.

THE IMPORTANCE OF TIMELINE IN THE SALES PROCESS

Timing can be as crucial as the product or service itself. A clear understanding of the client's deadline allows:

- **Prioritize leads:** Focusing efforts on leads with more immediate deadlines can optimize the sales flow and improve overall efficiency.

- **Personalize proposals:** Adapting your proposal to meet the client's temporal needs can differentiate you from the competition.

- **Manage expectations:** Aligning expectations between you and the client regarding deadlines avoids misunderstandings and builds a foundation of trust.

HOW TO DETERMINE THE CLIENT'S TIMELINE

- **Direct questions:** Start the conversation about deadlines by directly asking the customer when they expect to implement the solution or make the purchase. Be specific with your questions to get clear answers.

- **Understand the decision process:** Understanding how the decision process works in the customer organization can give you insights into typical purchasing and implementation timelines.

- **Identify trigger events:** Specific events, such as the end of a contract with a current supplier or an important project, can determine the deadline for decision making. Identify these events to better understand the customer's timeline.

- **Use CRM tools:** CRM tools can help you track and analyze time-related information from past decisions, providing a basis for predicting future behavior.

ADAPTING YOUR SALES STRATEGY TO THE CUSTOMER'S TIMELINE

Once you have an understanding of the customer's deadline, it's time to adapt your sales strategy to meet that timeline:

- **Speed up communication:** For leads with tight deadlines, step up communication and offer quick responses to their queries.

- **Offer agile solutions**: For customers who need solutions in a short period of time, highlight the agility and ease of implementation of your product or service.

- **Long-term planning:** For longer-term leads, maintain the relationship through regular communications, providing relevant information and ongoing value until the time to purchase approaches.

Understanding and aligning yourself with the customer's timeline is fundamental to sales success. However, effective application of the BANT method is not limited to understanding each component in isolation; it's also about integrating them cohesively and adapting them to different contexts and sales scenarios.

In the next chapter, " **APPLYING BANT IN DIFFERENT SALES SCENARIO** ", we will explore how the BANT method can be adapted and applied not only in B2B sales, but also in B2C scenarios, startups, and in contexts that demand consultative selling approaches. This chapter will equip you with practical insights to maximize the effectiveness of the BANT method, no matter what sales scenario you find yourself in.

Get ready to expand your understanding and application of BANT by adapting your strategies to meet the unique needs of each customer and sales scenario. Let's move forward together, as each interaction is an opportunity to learn, adapt and improve our lead qualification techniques.

APPLYING BANT IN DIFFERENT SALES SCENARIO

Now that we've explored the pillars of the BANT method (Budget, Authority , Need , Timeline), it's time to see how these concepts apply in different sales scenarios. Each context – whether B2B (Business to Business), B2C (Business to Consumer), startups or consultative sales – requires adaptation and a specific understanding of how to apply BANT effectively. This chapter will help you navigate these variations, ensuring you can maximize the effectiveness of your lead qualification strategies, regardless of the scenario.

B2B: COMPLEXITY AND MULTIPLE DECISION MAKERS

In B2B sales, the decision process often involves multiple stakeholders, each with their own needs and authority within the organization. Here, the " Authority " component of BANT is particularly critical. The key is to identify and engage all relevant influencers and decision-makers:

- **Map the organizational structure:** Understand who the main decision-makers and influencers are. Use tools such as stakeholder maps to visualize the influence network.

- **Tailor the message to different interests:** Personalize your communication to address each stakeholder's specific needs and concerns.

B2C: FOCUS ON NEED AND TIMELINE

In B2C sales, sales cycles tend to be shorter, and the decision often rests with the individual or family. Here, the " Need " and "Timeline" components are vital. It's important to quickly capture consumer interest and adapt your approach to meet their immediate needs and purchase timing:

- **Create compelling messages:** Target your messages to solve specific consumer needs or wants.

- **Agility in follow-up:** Respond quickly to queries and be proactive in follow-up, aligning your actions with the consumer's sense of urgency.

STARTUPS: FLEXIBILITY AND INNOVATION

Startups operate in a rapidly changing environment and often sell innovative or disruptive products. Here, the challenge is to educate the market while qualifying leads. The " Need " component takes on a new dimension, where you may need to create or identify a need that the customer has not yet recognized:

- **Educate your audience:** Provide valuable information that highlights the need for your product or service, even if the customer is not yet actively looking for a solution.

- **Demonstrate unique value:** Emphasize how your offering is different and superior to traditional or existing solutions.

CONSULTATIVE SALES: BUILDING RELATIONSHIPS

In consultative sales, the focus is on building a trusting relationship with the customer, deeply understanding their needs and offering personalized solutions. Here, " Need " and " Authority " are critical, as you need to understand exactly what the customer needs and ensure you are communicating with the right person:

- **Develop a dialogue:** Establish an open conversation to explore the customer's needs in depth, acting more like a consultant than a salesperson.

- **Solution Focus:** Show how your solution can solve your customer's specific problems by customizing your offering to meet their unique needs.

INTEGRATING BANT INTO YOUR SALES PROCESS

Regardless of the sales scenario, integrating the BANT method into your process requires practice and adaptation. Consider BANT as a flexible guide, not a rigid set of rules. The ability to adapt each element of BANT to the specific context of your lead is what sets successful sales professionals apart.

Now that we understand how to apply BANT in various sales scenarios, the next chapter, " **EFFECTIVE COMMUNICATION USING BANT** ", will focus on how you can communicate your value and differentiator, using the information collected through BANT to speak directly to the customer's needs. This chapter will be crucial to turning qualifications into conversions by teaching you how to use BANT not just as a qualification tool, but as a powerful communication strategy.

Get ready to deepen your communication and sales skills by using BANT to create more meaningful connections with your customers and boost your results. Let us advance together on this journey of learning and success.

EFFECTIVE COMMUNICATION USING BANT

Mastering the BANT method is more than just a way to qualify leads; It is also a powerful communication strategy. In this chapter, we'll explore how you can use the information collected through BANT to communicate your value and differentiator effectively, ensuring your message resonates directly with customer needs and expectations. The art of effective communication, when aligned with a deep understanding of BANT criteria, can transform potential customers into long-term partners.

UNDERSTANDING THE POWER OF COMMUNICATION AT BANT

Each element of BANT offers valuable insights that can be used to improve your communication:

- **Budget:** Knowing the client's budget allows you to adjust your proposal to suit financial limitations, highlighting the value that your solution offers in terms of cost-benefit.

- **Authority** : Understanding who makes decisions allows you to tailor your message to address the decision makers' specific concerns and goals.

- **Need** : Identifying customer needs helps focus your communication on the solutions and benefits that matter most to them.

- **Timeline:** Knowing the customer's timeline allows you to present your solution as the most viable option to meet their urgent needs.

STRATEGIES FOR EFFECTIVE COMMUNICATION

- **Adapt your message:** Use the information obtained by BANT to shape your message so that it speaks directly to the customer's pain points. For example, if budget is a concern, emphasize return on investment (ROI) or flexible financing options.

- **Create urgency with the timeline:** When you know the

customer has an immediate need, use this to create a sense of urgency. Show how your solution can be quickly implemented to meet this need, highlighting the efficiency and agility of your process.

- **Use authority to build credibility:** When communicating with decision makers, use data, case studies and testimonials to build credibility. Show how other companies, preferably in similar situations, have benefited from your solution.

- **Customize to need:** Talk about specific features of your product or service that meet identified needs. Personalization not only shows that you understand what the customer needs, but it also increases the relevance of your offer.

COMMUNICATION AS A COMPETITIVE DIFFERENCE

In a saturated market, the ability to communicate effectively is a crucial competitive differentiator. Use the information collected through BANT to not only qualify leads, but also to:

- **Establish emotional connections:** In addition to the technical aspects, it is important that your communication touches emotional points, creating a deeper connection with the customer.

- **Demonstrate understanding and empathy:** Show that you truly understand the customer's needs and challenges, and are here to help.

- **Position yourself as a trusted advisor:** More than a salesperson, you are a partner who offers solutions based on a clear understanding of the customer's needs.

Now that we understand how to use BANT to improve our communication, the next chapter will focus on " **OVERCOMING OBJECTIONS WITH THE HELP OF BANT** ". This chapter will be essential in helping you anticipate and effectively respond to any hesitations your customers may have, utilizing the deep understanding gained through BANT. Preparing to overcome objections is not only a crucial step in the sales process; It's also an opportunity to reinforce the value of your solution and solidify the customer's confidence in your proposition.

We move forward together on this journey, armed with powerful communication strategies that transform simple interactions into lasting relationships and successful sales.

OVERCOMING OBJECTIONS WITH THE HELP OF BANT

Overcoming objections is a fundamental skill in any sales professional's arsenal. However, instead of seeing objections as barriers, you can see them as opportunities to deepen your understanding of customer needs and reinforce the value of your solution. In this chapter, we will explore how the BANT method can be a powerful tool for anticipating and overcoming these objections, transforming doubts into confidence and hesitation into commitment.

UNDERSTANDING OBJECTIONS THROUGH BANT

Objections generally fall into one or more BANT categories: Budget, Authority , Need , and Timeline. Identifying the nature of the objection can help you apply the right strategy to overcome it:

- **Budget:** "It's very expensive." This objection indicates concerns about cost. Use your understanding of the client's budget to discuss value, ROI and flexible payment options.

- **Authority :** "I need to consult with the team." When the objection is about authority, it means you may not be speaking to the final decision maker. Use this as an opportunity to involve all decision makers in the process.

- **Need :** "I don't see how this fits into our operation." This suggests a disconnect between your solution and the customer's perceived needs. Reiterate your understanding of their needs and how your solution meets them.

- **Timeline:** "Now is not a good time." This objection points to timing. Offer flexibility in the implementation timeline or highlight the urgency of resolving the issue now.

STRATEGIES TO OVERCOME OBJECTIONS

- **Reinforce value:** For budget-related objections, emphasize the added value your solution offers, including the potential for long-term savings or increased efficiency.

- **Demonstrate flexibility:** Showing that you are willing

to work within the client's constraints, whether through customized payment plans or adapting the solution to better fit their needs, can help overcome budget and timeline objections.

- **Educate about the need:** Use data, case studies and testimonials to educate the customer about the need for your solution. Showing how other companies have benefited can help overcome inertia and skepticism.

- **Make it easy to commit:** For customers hesitant to make a decision, offer options that reduce perceived risk, such as warranties, exceptional after-sales support, or a trial version.

- **Use questions to reverse the objection:** Use strategic questions to understand the root of the objection and turn it into an opportunity to provide more information. For example, if the objection is price, ask: "What aspect of our product do you think does not justify the investment?" This may reveal misunderstandings that you can clarify.

VIEWING OBJECTIONS AS OPPORTUNITIES

Every objection is an opportunity to deepen your relationship with the customer. By overcoming objections with skill and empathy, you demonstrate your commitment to finding the best solution to the customer's needs, building a solid foundation of trust and credibility.

Overcoming objections is just one part of the sales process. In the next chapter, " **INTEGRATING BANT WITH OTHER SALES STRATEGIES** ", we will explore how BANT can be combined with other sales techniques and methodologies to create an even more holistic and effective sales approach. This chapter will provide insights into how you can enhance your overall sales strategy by utilizing BANT as a complementary tool to not only qualify leads but also successfully close sales.

Get ready to expand your repertoire of sales strategies by integrating the BANT method with other approaches to maximize your success in any sales scenario. We move forward together, equipped with the tools and knowledge needed to turn every sales interaction into a successful opportunity.

INTEGRATING BANT WITH OTHER SALES STRATEGIES

Now that we've mastered the BANT method and learned how to overcome objections using this framework, it's time to explore how we can integrate BANT with other sales strategies and techniques to create a more robust and holistic approach. This chapter focuses on expanding your view of how BANT can complement other sales methodologies, helping you improve your overall sales effectiveness, from lead generation to closing deals.

COMPLEMENTING BANT WITH INBOUND MARKETING

Inbound Marketing focuses on attracting customers through relevant and useful content rather than direct interruptions. Integrating BANT with Inbound Marketing allows you to qualify content-generated leads, identifying which ones are ready for a more direct sales approach:

> **- Use content to educate on needs and solutions:** Articles, e-books and webinars can help set the stage by addressing prospects' "Needs" and educating them on potential solutions.

> **- Evaluate engagement to determine budget and timeline:** A lead's level of engagement with your content can give clues about your budget and timeline, allowing for a more personalized approach.

SIN (Situation, Implication, Need-Payment) and BANT

The SIN methodology complements BANT by focusing first on the customer's situation, then on the implications of not resolving a specific problem, and finally on the need to pay to resolve that problem. Integrating SIN and BANT offers a complete approach that starts with a broad understanding of the customer landscape and ends with qualification based on specific criteria:

> **- Match situation and need for accurate diagnosis:** Use the "Situation" phase to collect detailed information that can help identify the customer's "Needs" more accurately.

- **Link implications to budget and timeline:** The "Implications" of not acting (or acting too late) can be used to discuss the necessary "Budget" and "Timeline" for implementation.

Integrating BANT with Consultative Selling

Consultative selling focuses on creating value and building strong relationships, guiding the customer through the purchasing process with a high level of personalization. BANT can be integrated to ensure consultative selling efforts are efficiently targeted:

- **Use BANT to further personalize consulting:** Information about the client's budget, authority, needs and timeline allows you to tailor your sales consultations to address specific points of interest and concern.

- **Authority and needs to build customized solutions:** Understanding who has the decision-making authority and what the specific needs are helps you shape your value proposition so that it resonates more deeply with the customer.

BANT and Social Selling

Social Selling is the process of developing relationships as part of the sales process, primarily using social media. BANT can be integrated with Social Selling to qualify leads more effectively:

- **Identify BANT Signals in Social Interactions:** Comments, posts and interactions on social networks can provide valuable insights into the budget, authority, needs and timeline of potential customers.

- **Use BANT insights to personalize social interactions:** Tailor your messaging and interactions based on what you've learned about the lead, using Social Selling to directly address BANT criteria.

As we integrate BANT with various sales strategies, it is equally important to explore the available tools and technologies that can support and enhance this integration. In the next chapter, " **TOOLS AND TECHNOLOGIES TO SUPPORT BANT** ", we will dive into digital solutions that can facilitate the application of BANT in the lead qualification process, from CRMs and marketing automation platforms to data analysis and artificial intelligence tools.

Be prepared to discover how technology can simplify and enhance your application of the BANT method, allowing you to focus on what really matters: building meaningful relationships with your customers and closing more sales. Let us move forward together on this journey to transform not only the way we sell, but also how we create lasting value for our customers.

TOOLS AND TECHNOLOGIES TO SUPPORT BANT

Effective application of the BANT method in your sales strategies can be significantly improved with the use of modern tools and technologies. This chapter explores a variety of digital solutions that can make it easier to qualify leads, collect data needed for BANT, and personalize your sales approaches. From Customer Relationship Management (CRM) systems to marketing automation platforms and artificial intelligence tools, the sales technology ecosystem offers powerful capabilities to maximize the efficiency and effectiveness of your sales strategies.

CUSTOMER RELATIONSHIP MANAGEMENT (CRM)

CRM systems are essential for managing lead and customer information, allowing effective monitoring throughout the sales cycle. They provide a solid foundation for applying the BANT method, storing details about the customer's budget, key people with decision-making authority, specific needs and timeline for purchase.

- **Key Features:** Easily record and access information about customer interactions, manage tasks and follow-up reminders, and analyze the sales pipeline to better understand where to focus your efforts.

MARKETING AUTOMATION PLATFORMS

Marketing automation can play a crucial role in qualifying leads through BANT, nurturing leads with personalized content based on their past interactions and collected data.

- **How to Use:** Use segmented email campaigns to address leads' specific needs, score leads based on their engagement to gauge budget and interest, and automate follow-up based on lead behavior that suggests a change in your purchase timeline.

DATA ANALYSIS AND ARTIFICIAL INTELLIGENCE TOOLS

Data analytics and AI solutions can provide deep insights into lead behavior, helping to forecast budgets, identify decision makers, understand unexpressed needs, and estimate purchase timelines.

- **Implementation: Apply** machine algorithms learning to analyze the history of interactions and transactions, identifying patterns that indicate the lead's readiness to buy. Use AI-powered chatbots to gather preliminary information about BANT during initial website interactions.

SOCIAL SELLING AND SALES INTELLIGENCE TOOLS

Social selling, supported by sales intelligence tools, allows salespeople to connect with potential customers on social media, collecting valuable information that can be used for BANT qualification.

- **Advantages:** Monitor discussions and posts on social platforms to identify leads with specific needs, recognize authorities within organizations and better understand the ideal timing for engagement.

CONSIDERATIONS WHEN CHOOSING TECHNOLOGIES

When selecting tools and technologies to support the application of the BANT method, consider:

- **Integration with other tools:** The ability to integrate with other platforms in use by your sales and marketing team is crucial for an efficient workflow.

- **Scalability:** Choose solutions that can grow with your company, adapting to changes in the volume of leads and the complexity of sales.

- **Usability:** Intuitive tools that are easy to adopt by the team are essential to ensure that they will be effectively used.

With the right tools in hand, the next step is to ensure your team is well trained and prepared to use the BANT method and associated technologies with maximum efficiency. In the next chapter, **"TRAINING AND SKILLS DEVELOPMENT IN BANT"**, we will cover strategies for empowering your sales team, ensuring they are equipped not only with the tools, but also the knowledge and skills needed to effectively apply BANT in your sales interactions.

Get ready to invest in developing your team, as combining enhanced skills with advanced technology is the key to transforming the lead qualification process and driving sales success.

TRAINING AND SKILLS DEVELOPMENT IN BANT

The effectiveness of the BANT method does not only depend on the strategy or technological tools used, but crucially, on the level of skill of the sales team in applying this method. Therefore, investing in the training and ongoing development of these skills is vital to maximizing sales success. This chapter focuses on effective strategies for training your team on the nuances of BANT, ensuring everyone is able to identify, qualify, and convert leads more efficiently.

FUNDAMENTALS OF BANT TRAINING

- **Deep understanding of each component:** The first step is to ensure the team has a solid understanding of each aspect of BANT: Budget, Authority, Need, and Timeline. This includes recognizing how each of these elements influences the purchasing decision process and how to identify them during interactions with customers.

- **Simulations and role-playing:** Using simulations and role-playing exercises can be extremely effective in training the team to apply BANT in real situations. These activities help develop practical skills such as asking the right questions to discover information about BANT and how to appropriately respond to customer objections.

- **Use of technological tools:** Train your team not only in the theoretical aspect of BANT, but also in the effective use of technological tools that support the application of this method. This includes CRM, marketing automation, data analytics, and sales intelligence platforms.

ADVANCED TRAINING STRATEGIES

- **Continuous training:** BANT training should not be a one-time event, but an ongoing process. This can include regular update sessions, workshops and webinars to keep the team informed about best practices and new trends in sales.

- **Feedback and coaching:** Implementing a system of

constructive feedback and individualized coaching can help identify specific areas of improvement for each team member and provide personalized guidance for skill development.

- Sales certifications: Encouraging or even subsidizing the obtaining of professional sales certifications for your team can significantly increase the level of competence and confidence in applying BANT and other sales strategies.

MEASURING TRAINING SUCCESS

- Performance evaluation: Use specific performance metrics to evaluate the impact of training on the sales process. This can include qualified lead conversion rate, average sales cycle, and customer satisfaction.

- Participant feedback: Getting direct feedback from the team on the effectiveness of the training can provide valuable insights for future adjustments and improvements.

With a well-trained team equipped with the necessary skills to apply the BANT method effectively, the next step is to put this knowledge into practice. In the next chapter, " **30-DAY ACTION PLAN TO IMPLEMENT BANT** ", we will present a step-by-step guide that will help you and your team integrate BANT into your sales routines, establishing clear goals and specific actions to improve lead qualification and increase conversions.

Get ready to embark on a structured implementation journey, turning theory into practice and maximizing your team's sales potential with the power of BANT.

30-DAY ACTION PLAN TO IMPLEMENT BANT

Once you've equipped your team with the knowledge and tools needed to effectively apply the BANT method, it's time to put this theory into practice. This chapter presents a detailed 30-day action plan designed to integrate BANT into your sales routines and significantly improve lead qualification and conversion rates. By following this plan, you and your team will be on the right path to achieving more efficient and predictable sales results.

WEEK 1: GOAL SETTING AND PREPARATION

Day 1-2: BANT Fundamentals Review

- Conduct a review session with the team to ensure understanding of the BANT method.

- Discuss practical examples and scenarios where BANT can be applied.

Day 3: Setting specific goals

- Establish clear goals for implementing BANT, including desired increases in lead qualification and conversion.

Day 4-5: Preparation of materials and tools

- Ensure all CRM tools and sales technologies are configured to support BANT data collection and analysis.

- Develop BANT-based scripts and checklists to guide staff through customer interactions.

WEEK 2: IMPLEMENTATION AND PRACTICE

Day 6-10: Focus on practical application

- The team must begin actively applying the BANT method in all sales interactions.

- Use role- playing and simulations to reinforce the use of BANT in real situations.

- Start a logbook or recording system to track the application of BANT and the results obtained.

WEEK 3: ANALYSIS AND ADJUSTMENTS

Day 11-17: Monitoring and analyzing results

- Monitor sales interactions using CRM and analytics tools to evaluate BANT effectiveness.

- Gather team feedback on challenges and successes in applying the method.

Day 18-20: Adjustments based on feedback

- Based on the data collected and feedback from the team, make adjustments to the approaches and tools used.

- Conduct additional training sessions if necessary to address any identified gaps.

WEEK 4: CONSOLIDATION AND FUTURE PLANNING

Day 21-24: Reinforcement of BANT application

- Continue to emphasize the importance of BANT in daily sales routines.

- Share success stories and best practices within the team to motivate and inspire.

Day 25-27: Evaluation of results

- Evaluate progress against the goals established at the beginning of the action plan.

- Identify areas of success and those that still require improvement.

Day 28-30: Planning for the future

- Based on the results and learnings from the month, develop a plan for continued BANT implementation.

- Establish long-term goals for the continued integration of BANT into sales strategies.

By the end of this 30-day action plan, your team will not only have a deeper understanding of the BANT method, they will also have experienced its practical application in real-world sales situations. The important thing is to maintain momentum, continuing to refine and adapt sales strategies based on BANT and the feedback collected. Remember, sales excellence is an ongoing journey of learning, adapting and growing. With BANT as one of your core tools, you are well positioned to maximize sales success and build lasting relationships with your customers.

As we turn the final page of this journey together, I sincerely hope that the learnings shared here have touched your heart and sparked new perspectives. If this book has brought you any value, I kindly ask that you take a few moments to leave a review on Amazon. Your words not only help me grow and hone my craft, but they also guide other readers in their quests for knowledge and inspiration. Your opinion is a valuable gift, both for me and for the community of readers looking for stories that transform. I sincerely thank you for sharing this journey with me and I hope we can meet again in the pages of a new adventure.

REGINALDO OSNILDO

Hello, I'm Reginaldo Osnildo, author and innovator in the areas of sales, technology, and communication strategies. My experience ranges from the academic environment, as a professor and researcher at the University of Southern Santa Catarina, to practice as a strategist at Grupo Catarinense de Rádios. With a PhD in sales narratives and digital convergence, and a master's degree in storytelling and social imaginary, I bring my readers a unique fusion of theory and practice. My goal is to provide knowledge in a simple, practical and didactic language, encouraging direct application in personal and professional life.

Yours sincerely

Reginaldo Osnildo

+55 48 991913865

reginaldoosnildo@gmail.com

www.ingramcontent.com/pod-product-compliance
Lightning Source LLC
Chambersburg PA
CBHW051535240526
45471CB00020B/2844